Animal Migrations

Bat Migration

by Carolyn Bennett Fraiser

FOCUS READERS®

BEACON

www.focusreaders.com

Focus Readers is distributed by North Star Editions:
sales@northstareditions.com | 888-417-0195

Produced for Focus Readers by Red Line Editorial.

Photographs ©: Shutterstock Images, cover, 1, 7, 13, 14–15, 16, 22, 25, 27, 29; Nick Garbutt/Nature Picture Library/Alamy, 4; Rick & Nora Bowers/Alamy, 8, 18; Michael Durham/Nature Picture Library/ Alamy, 11; Jack Milchanowski/Papilio/Alamy, 21

Library of Congress Cataloging-in-Publication Data
Names: Fraiser, Carolyn Bennett, author.
Title: Bat migration / by Carolyn Bennett Fraiser.
Description: Lake Elmo, MN : Focus Readers, [2024] | Series: Animal
  migrations | Includes bibliographical references and index. | Audience:
  Grades 2-3
Identifiers: LCCN 2023005393 (print) | LCCN 2023005394 (ebook) | ISBN
  9781637396049 (hardcover) | ISBN 9781637396612 (paperback) | ISBN
  9781637397725 (ebook pdf) | ISBN 9781637397183 (hosted ebook)
Subjects: LCSH: Bats--Migration--Juvenile literature.
Classification: LCC QL737.C5 F73 2024 (print) | LCC QL737.C5 (ebook) |
  DDC 599.4--dc23/eng/20230302
LC record available at https://lccn.loc.gov/2023005393
LC ebook record available at https://lccn.loc.gov/2023005394

Printed in the United States of America
Mankato, MN
082023

About the Author

Carolyn Bennet Fraiser has been an avid animal lover since she was a child. An author of several books for children, she loves learning new things about animals and nature. She currently lives in western North Carolina, where she writes for nonprofit organizations and adopts as many rescued animals as her husband will allow.

Table of Contents

Chapter 1

Migration of Millions

Straw-colored fruit bats live across much of Africa. But every October, millions of these bats fly to the same place. They **migrate** to a national park in Zambia. There, heavy rains cause trees to bloom.

 Bats are the only mammals that can fly.

The bats arrive just in time to eat ripe fruit.

During the day, the bats hang upside down in trees. They begin to eat when the sun sets. In a single night, the bats can eat twice their weight in fruit.

By December, the fruit is gone. Now the bats have enough strength

Fun Fact

Straw-colored fruit bats take part in the world's largest **mammal** migration.

 Straw-colored fruit bats roost in trees.

to fly again. They must search for more fruit across Africa. Many will migrate hundreds of miles. They will return to Zambia next October.

Chapter 2

Why Bats Migrate

Bats live all around the world. Many **species** migrate during the spring and fall. Some travel to areas where they can **hibernate**. Others just need to find more food.

 Hoary bats live across much of North America.

Some species live far from the **equator**. Migration is most common in these bats. They often have a summer **roost** and a winter roost. Changing temperatures tell them when it is time to move.

The hoary bat is a common species in the Americas. During the summer, hoary bats live in forests across North America. In the fall, they migrate to warmer areas in the United States and Mexico. During the winter, hoary bats hibernate.

Hoary bats eat mostly moths. They also eat insects such as beetles and mosquitoes.

They need warm places to stay.

So, some rest in caves. Others go into mines.

Other species stay active all year. Many of these bats live near the equator. There, it is warm all year. However, some of these bats still migrate. That is because they have to find food. Some species eat insects or fruit. Others drink **nectar** from flowers. But sometimes

Fun Fact

Female bats often migrate farther than males. Then, females spend the summers together in large groups.

 A lesser long-nosed bat drinks nectar from an agave flower.

there is not enough food in one area. When food runs out, the bats migrate. They move to places where there is more to eat.

Tracking Migration

The Nathusius' pipistrelle lives across much of Europe. This bat weighs less than 0.5 ounces (14.2 grams). Scientists wanted to track its migration. So, they placed tiny metal bands on many bats. That way, scientists could find out how far the bats traveled.

In 2009, a bat was found in France. It had a band that said "Russia." The bat had traveled more than 1,500 miles (2,400 kilometers). That was the longest bat migration ever recorded.

The Nathusius' pipistrelle tends to live near trees.

Chapter 3

Long-Distance Migration

Some bats make their homes in deep caves. These caves stay the same temperature all year. That means the bats do not have to travel far to hibernate.

 Bats hang upside down when they sleep.

 The silver-haired bat migrates long distances in North America.

However, other bats do not live in deep caves. They need warmer temperatures when they hibernate. So, many species fly hundreds of miles. These bats have long wings with pointed tips. This wing shape helps the bats travel far.

Bats fly at night. As they travel, they use echolocation. The bats make sounds. The sounds echo off nearby objects. The bats hear the echoes. That helps them find their way in the dark. It also helps them find food.

Most bats also have a homing **instinct**. It helps them find their roosts. They often return to the same place year after year.

Migrating a long distance can be hard. So, bats need to store energy before they leave. Most bats eat a lot during the summer or fall. They also need to eat during the trip. For this reason, bats often follow insects when they migrate.

Mexican long-nosed bats eat nectar from agave plants. Every

Fun Fact

Thousands of Mexican long-nosed bats can roost at a single site.

 Mexican long-nosed bats are endangered because of habitat loss.

spring, the bats travel from Mexico to the United States as these plants flower. Eventually, the plants go out of bloom. Then the bats leave. They fly hundreds of miles back to central Mexico.

Chapter 4

Threats to Migration

Bats face many dangers. Humans are one of the biggest threats. Some people kill bats. They might be afraid of them. Or they might think that bats are pests. In addition, humans destroy many bat habitats.

Habitat loss has forced many bats to live closer to humans.

They cut down trees. They block caves. Then the bats have no place to roost. And in some cases, they have no food.

Humans cause problems for bat migration, too. Outdoor lights can confuse bats. Bats can lose track of migration routes. Wind turbines are also a problem. Bats often fly into the spinning blades. Hundreds of thousands of bats die each year.

Climate change is also affecting bat migration. Bats might not arrive

 Wind turbines may kill more than 800,000 bats every year.

when insects are plentiful. Females

may not find enough food to feed

their young.

Bats are beneficial. They eat insects that harm plants or carry diseases. For example, Mexican free-tailed bats eat more than 60 kinds of insects. That helps control insect populations. Bats save farmers billions of dollars every year. Without the bats, insects would ruin many crops.

Fun Fact

Some bats can eat up to 600 insects per hour.

 Pallas's long-tongued bats feed on nectar.

Bats are also good **pollinators**. They spread the pollen of many flowering plants. And they drop seeds when they poop. In this way, bats help plants grow and spread.

FOCUS ON
Bat Migration

Write your answers on a separate piece of paper.

1. Write a paragraph describing the main ideas of Chapter 4.

2. What type of bat migration do you think is most impressive? Why?

3. Which bat has the longest migration?
    A. Mexican free-tailed bats
    B. hoary bats
    C. Nathusius' pipistrelle

4. Why might deep caves stay the same temperature all year?
    A. caves are not affected by weather on the surface
    B. caves are heated from fires deep below the ground
    C. caves stay closed during the winter months

5. What does **habitats** mean in this book?

*In addition, humans destroy many bat **habitats**. They cut down trees. They block caves.*

   A. things that animals eat
   B. places where animals live
   C. parts of animals' bodies

6. What does **beneficial** mean in this book?

*Bats are **beneficial**. They eat insects that harm plants or carry diseases.*

   A. good or helpful
   B. bad or unhealthy
   C. uncommon

Answer key on page 32.

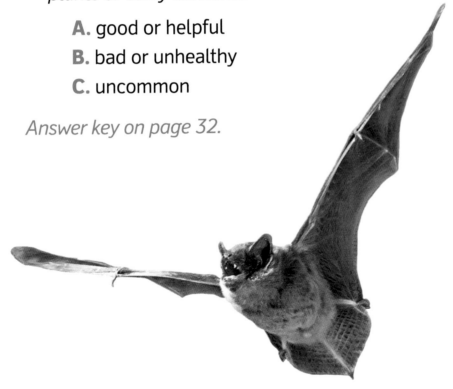

Glossary

climate change
A human-caused global crisis involving long-term changes in Earth's temperature and weather patterns.

equator
An imaginary line that runs around the middle of Earth.

hibernate
To save energy by resting or sleeping during a season.

instinct
A behavior that is natural instead of learned.

mammal
An animal that has hair and produces milk for its young.

migrate
To move from one region to another.

nectar
A sweet liquid released by plants.

pollinators
Animals that spread pollen. This powder creates new plants.

roost
A place where bats rest and raise their young.

species
Groups of animals or plants that are alike and can breed with one another.

To Learn More

BOOKS

Bassier, Emma. *Bats*. Minneapolis: Abdo Publishing, 2020.

MacCarald, Clara. *Migrating to Survive*. Minneapolis: Abdo Publishing, 2023.

Mattern, Joanne. *What's So Scary About Bats?* South Egremont, MA: Red Chair Press, 2023.

NOTE TO EDUCATORS

Visit **www.focusreaders.com** to find lesson plans, activities, links, and other resources related to this title.

Index

C
caves, 11, 17–18, 24
climate change, 24–25

E
echolocation, 19

H
habitat loss, 23–24
hibernation, 9, 11, 17–18
hoary bat, 10–11

I
insects, 12, 20, 25–26

M
Mexican free-tailed bats, 26
Mexican long-nosed bats, 20–21
Mexico, 10, 21

N
Nathusius' pipistrelle, 14
nectar, 12, 20
North America, 10, 21

P
pollinators, 27

S
straw-colored fruit bats, 5–7

U
United States, 10, 21

Z
Zambia, 5, 7

Answer Key: 1. Answers will vary; 2. Answers will vary; 3. C; 4. A; 5. B; 6. A